The Al-Nusra Front: The History of th
Affiliated with /

By Charles Rivei

The group's flag

About Charles River Editors

Charles River Editors is a boutique digital publishing company, specializing in bringing history back to life with educational and engaging books on a wide range of topics. Keep up to date with our new and free offerings with this 5 second sign up on our weekly mailing list, and visit Our Kindle Author Page to see other recently published Kindle titles.

We make these books for you and always want to know our readers' opinions, so we encourage you to leave reviews and look forward to publishing new and exciting titles each week.

Introduction

A Voice of America picture of Al-Nusra Front supporters

The Al-Nusra Front

Since the Arab Spring uprising of 2011, reports of terrorist attacks around the world have flooded international media. Syria, a country about one and half times the size of Texas, has become the central battleground for many terrorist groups; those the world often focuses on and has heard much of--such as the Islamic State of Iraq and the Levant (also known as ISIS and Da'ash, but from here on referred to as ISIL)--and those the world rarely hears about and is unable to make distinctions between others--such as Jabhat Al-Nusra. Despite the lack of focused attention on its activities, Jabhat Al-Nusra (or, the Nusra Front as it is sometimes referred to) has built quite a reputation in Syria and the greater Middle East for its seemingly endless supply of weapons, ability to ally with strategic partners, and its peculiar mix of international, albeit notorious, supporters inside the country.

Jabhat Al-Nusra's formal name is, "Jabhat Al-Nusra li-Ahl al-Sham," or, the "Victorious Support Front for the People of Sham (or, Syria)" and the group first emerged on the international scene in early 2012 as a localized Syrian affiliate of Al-Qaeda in Iraq. The group has carried out numerous terrorist attacks and kidnappings, and has been involved in a variety of battles against Bashar Assad's Syrian government forces as well as against other anti-government factions such as ISIL. The complexity of the Syrian Civil War is most definitely reflected in the complexity of the groups fighting for power within and around its borders; Jabhat Al-Nusra is no exception. The group's relationship with ISIL, Al-Qaeda, and the other militant factions within Syria is complicated and appears often conflictual: as of the time of this writing, Jabhat Al-Nusra had announced its split from Al-Qaeda in Iraq (AQI) but analysts believe this is nothing more than a re-branding technique to attract all fighting elements in Syria to be under its own umbrella of control.

Abu Muhammad Al-Julani (real name, Ahmad Hussein Al-Shar'a) is currently the top leader of Jabhat Al-Nusra and one of its founding members. Al-Julani boasts a long career with jihadist groups in the region and his ties to Al-Qaeda are particularly strong which has served Al-Nusra very well over the last few years, especially when it comes to drawing upon resources and increasing recruitment for the cause. Al-Julani and Jabhat Al-Nusra aim to continue to increase recruitment and integrate all Syrian revolutionary factions into one larger group, thereby beginning the establishment of their own version of an Islamic caliphate in Syria. While their idea to build a caliphate in Syria is certainly not unique, their approach to this effort has most recently centered on finding consensus among warring factions to maximize efforts against Bashar Assad's regime forces as well as experimenting with efforts of control in occupied cities around Syria.

The international community's response to the Syria Civil War has been quite disorganized. The United States was quick to support the protester movements across the region during the Arab Spring which put Syrian President Bashar Assad on high alert. As the war commenced inside Syria, Russia was quick to rush to Assad's defense and aid both inside the country and to the international community more generally. This situation pitted the U.S. and Russia against each other once again which left the Syrian people in between. Jabhat Al-Nusra took this as an opportunity to fill in the gap where the world's superpowers failed them. Not only is Al-Nusra attempting to gain legitimacy within the country, they want to show the world they are the only force fighting for the Sunnis of Syria. From the summer of 2014 to 2016, the U.S.-led coalition has focused much of its effort on destroying the brutal ISIL whose territory encompasses parts of both Iraq and Syria. Al-Nusra has capitalized on ISIL's time in the spotlight and carved its own niche among Syrians, developing relationships and carrying out small scale battles against the Assad regime and rival rebel militant groups around the country. This has been particularly attractive to countries like Turkey and Qatar, whose feel their own position in the region may shift depending on the outcome of the war and the United States' changing relationship with Iran. Al-Nusra certainly appears more appealing than ISIL. In late July 2016, Al-Nusra evolved once more by changing its name to Jabhat Fatah Al-Sham and officially cutting ties with Al-Qaeda. According to analysts, this move is just another step in a long-term effort for Al-Nusra to make itself seem different than the other groups it competes with in the region and to shake loose Al-Qaeda's baggage.

The Al-Nusra Front: The History of the Syrian Rebel Group Formerly Affiliated with Al-Qaeda explores the development of a highly specialized terrorist group, one that adapts quickly to situations on the ground as the conflict progresses and learns from other groups mistakes. Al-Nusra is relatively agile and seemingly less vicious than ISIL, which is why it both attracts and repels the international community. Examining Al-Nusra's bridging of online and offline battlefields and its internal structure allows readers to understand how this group developed so rapidly in the war. Understanding how Syrian civilians live under Al-Nusra controls allows readers to understand the similarities and differences with ISIL, whose caliphate it is often compared to. These various components paint the picture of "Al-Nusra the terrorist group, but also one of the group as "Al-Nusra the Syrian defender." Along with pictures of important people, places, and events, you will learn about the Al-Nusra Front like never before.

The Al-Nusra Front: The History of the Syrian Rebel Group Formerly Affiliated with Al-Qaeda

Chapter 1: The Syrian Civil War

"First of all, you're talking about the president of the United States, not the president of Syria -- so he can only talk about his country. It is not legitimate for him to judge Syria. He doesn't have the right to tell the Syrian people who their president will be. Second, what he says doesn't have anything to do with the reality. He's been talking about the same thing -- that the president has to quit -- for a year and a half now. Has anything happened? Nothing has happened." – Bashar al-Assad

Late 2010 and early 2011 was a very tumultuous time in the Middle East. Waves of protesters took to the streets for days on end in Tunisia, Egypt, Bahrain, and Yemen. Syria was also one of these countries to suffer from a long period of instability, and of course it has since become the focal point of the multi-faceted conflicts roiling the region.

The primary grievance for most protesters in the region, during what has come to be known as the "Arab Spring," was a call for social justice and reforms which eventually turned into demands for regime change against long-standing dictatorships. While some of these Arab countries underwent rapid and immense changes in leadership, in most cases, the clashes among protesters and police were mostly infrequent during this time and did not amount to large-scale violence between the military and civilians.

Syrian President Bashar Assad, on the other hand, did not respond with as much restraint as other leaders in the region. As protester demands changed from a desire for social reforms to regime change, Assad began to blame foreign entities for the ensuing chaos. The theme of blaming foreigners for all internal problems is fairly common throughout the Middle East, particularly in dictatorship, since it attempts to absolve the country's leader from any guilt or wrongdoing. This notion of blaming foreign enemies eventually played well into Jabhat Al-Nusra's plan for localizing its activities, as it claims to be a native movement.

Assad

The Arab Spring officially began in December 2010 in Tunisia when a student and fruit vendor named Muhammad Bouazizi had his fruit cart confiscated by police who probably wanted a bribe (Lesch 2012, 45). Bouazizi reacted with the extreme form of protest of self-immolation, a suicide that led to protests fuelled by social media. The protests reached the capital of Tunis on January 13, 2011, and they ultimately forced Tunisia's dictator, Ben Ali, to flee to Saudi Arabia (Lesch 2012, 47).

The scene of angry street protests directed at a despotic leader was replayed in Egypt, and as the protests continued, Western pressure induced Egyptian dictator Hosni Mubarak to step down from the presidency just weeks after the events in Tunisia (Lesch 2012, 48). It seemed that no dictator in the Arabic speaking world was immune, and protests sprouted from the Gulf States to Morocco. Despots who had ruled for decades, including Ali, Mubarak, and Qaddafi in Libya, were eventually overthrown.

Although Syria witnessed anti-government protests similar to those in other countries during the Arab Spring, they were initially much smaller and not very organized (Lesch 2012, 53). The lack of large-scale protests initially in Syria can be attributed to its uniqueness as a nation among its Arabic speaking neighbors. The complex intelligence and police state apparatus in Syria no doubt contributed to stamping out many of the protests before they could grow into something much larger, but the personality and public perception of Bashar al-Assad is another factor that mitigated protests in Syria. Bashar was much less hated by his people than the other dictators who were toppled during the Arab Spring (Lesch 2012, 52). For example, Ali and Mubarak were viewed by many of their peoples as American stooges, while Qaddafi had rightly earned his reputation as an eccentric tyrant.

One of the more important and unique aspects of Syria that reduced the amount and intensity of initial protests there was its demographic composition. In the 21st century, Syria is a country comprised of many different religious sects and tribes; the Sunni Muslims are the majority, but the minority Shia and Christian sects form about 30% of the population, and they have traditionally been loyal to the al-Assad family, who they view as protectors (Lesch 2012, 51-52).

As the last two years have made clear, far worse has happened in Syria than mere protests. If the early Arab Spring protests never took hold in Syria, how did the country devolve into the current situation? The answer is a combination of Assad's hubris and his inability to understand tide of change in the Middle East. It is unknown whether or not if the protests would have been suppressed or fizzled out, but in March 2011, several schoolboys from the southwestern Syrian city of Deraa scribbled the words "down with the regime" in Arabic on a wall in their school (Lesch 2012, 55). In any other time the boys would have probably just been punished by the school authorities, but in the shadow of the Arab Spring the kids were arrested and tortured (Lesch 2012, 56). As a result of the children's incarceration and torture, their families protested in central Deraa on March 15, 2011, which then spread across Syria via social networking websites (Lesch 2012, 56). Ironically, these repressive tactics were being used the very same month *Vogue*'s puff piece on Asma was published, making clear the extent of the Assad family's propaganda attempts with the West and humiliating the magazine so badly that the article on Asma was quickly removed from their website. As Gawker's editor, John Cook, put it, "I think it's important that people are aware of how Vogue…felt about the Assads, and characterized the Assads. It came out almost exactly as the regime embarked on its campaign of murdering women and children...And now in the context of the United States possibly going to war with Syria, it's important for people to see how the magazine portrayed them... "

Bashar might have been able to stem the tide of the protests with conciliatory gestures, but his pride and ego got the best of him. Instead of admitting the mistakes his police agents made in the Deraa situation, Assad chose to blame outside sources and "conspiracies" for the protests and unrest. Bashar said in a speech to the Syrian People's Assembly on March 30, 2011: "Our enemies work every day in an organized, systemic and scientific manner in order to undermine

Syria's stability. We acknowledge that they had been smart in choosing very sophisticated tools in what they have done, but at the same time we realize that they have been stupid in choosing this country and this people, for such conspiracies do not work with our country or our people." (Lesch 2012, 76-77) Even late in 2012, with the civil war raging, Assad remained defiant when *Der Spiegel* asked if he was sorry about the way his supporters handled Deraa: "There were personal mistakes made by individuals. We all make mistakes. Even a president makes mistakes. But even if there were mistakes in the implementation, our decisions were still fundamentally the right ones."

Bashar's obstinate attitude toward the protesters took a violent turn when he gave his brother, Maher, a free hand to deal with them. Maher filled a role similar to his uncle Rifaat before he was exiled from Syria, as he was head of the Fourth Armored Division and the Republican Guard, which served to protect the regime (Lesch 2012, 105). Just as Bashar's father Hafez called in Rifaat to put down the Muslim Brotherhood insurgency in the late 1970's and early 1980s, Bashar appealed to Maher to suppress protests in Syria 30 years later, which he gladly did with equally brutal methods, often carried out personally (Lesch 2012, 105). The primary difference between the two situations was that the methods employed by Hafez and Rifaat ultimately proved to be successful, while those used by Bashar and Maher have apparently thrown Syria into a state of sectarian warfare.

Hafez al-Assad

Maher al-Assad

Rifaat al-Assad

One of the primary strengths of the Assad dynasty, the backing of the Alawite sect, also became one of the major reasons why Syria devolved into sectarian warfare. Most of the government and police forces who participated in the violent crackdowns against protesters were Alawites, while the majority of the opposition was from the Sunni community, which was portrayed by the Assad regime as fundamentalists (Lesch 2012, 106). Assad has used the fragmented sectarian demographic background of Syria to his advantage by arguing that if fundamentalist Sunnis came to power in Syria, it would mean bloodshed for the Alawites, Ishmailis, Druze, and Christians whom his family protected. After all, the Syrian minorities only needed to look at the persecution the Christian Copts of Egypt were experiencing in the wake of their Arab Spring (Lesch 2012, 107).

In April of 2011, Assad's regime commanded the Syrian Army to begin firing upon neighborhoods in Damascus and around Syria[1] to combat what they told the world were "terrorists" trying to bring the country down. This narrative of blaming Syria's instability on foreign-backed terrorists would come to shape the international conversation among states who believed that intervention in the civil war would be seen as an attack on sovereignty rather than support of revolutionary forces against a brutal dictator. As the attacks raged around the country, soldiers in the military began to defect from the army and form the Free Syrian Army.

Although Assad's tactic of dividing Syria's population may have initially helped him stay in power, it had the effect of deepening the sectarian conflict. Furthermore, as defectors from the Syrian army began to form the Free Syrian Army, Islamic militant jihadists also began to enter the war (Lesch 2012, 174-75). Although the Free Syrian Army is comprised of a lot of secular elements (British Broadcasting Company 2013, October 17), Assad's propaganda campaign has tirelessly depicted his enemies as Al-Qaeda connected terrorists, and he has portrayed a potential Free Syrian Army victory as genocide for Syria's Shia and Christian communities. The fear has prompted paramilitary Alawite gangs, known as *Shabihas* (ghosts in Arabic), to kill members of the opposition and Sunnis indiscriminately (Lesch 2012, 177). The situation in Syria has effectively evolved over the last nearly three years from one of protest to revolution and now finally to a sectarian civil war that shows no signs of ending. Perhaps not surprisingly, Assad has denied the Shabihas exist, even while justifying their existence: "There is nothing called 'Shabiha' in Syria. In many remote areas where there is no possibility for the army and police to go and rescue the people and defend them, people have bought arms and set up their own small forces to defend themselves against attacks by militants. Some of them have fought with the army, that's true. But they are not militias that have been created to support the president. At issue is their country, which they want to defend from al-Qaida."

Assad's branding of his enemies as foreign agents and terrorists has greatly helped him. In response to questions from *Der Spiegel* about the Syrian people wanting him gone, Assad said of his enemies, "Again, when you talk about factions, whether they are opposition or supporters, you have to ask yourself the question: Whom do they represent? Themselves or the country that made them? Are they speaking for the United States, the United Kingdom, France, Saudi Arabia and Qatar? My answer here has to be frank and straight to the point. This conflict has been brought to our country from abroad. These people are located abroad, they live in five-star hotels and they say and do what those countries tell them to do. But they have no grassroots in Syria." At the same time, he has cast his opponents as the very Al-Qaeda terrorists the West despises: "The whole problem wasn't about the president. What do killing innocents, explosions and the terrorism that al-Qaida is bringing to the country have to do with me being in office?"

Either way, resistance against the Syrian government and the instability continued to gradually

---

[1] Gattas, K. (2011, May 24). *US policy on Syria 'depends on success in Libya'*. Retrieved from BBC News: http://www.bbc.com/news/world-middle-east-13529923

grow and explode not only in Syria but along the borders in the neighboring countries of Iraq, Israel, Jordan, Lebanon, and Turkey. Like in many countries around world, the borders of Syria are porous, which makes it easier for people, weapons, and other resources to pass through. The Syrian Civil War and its resulting consequences have severely impacted the politics, economies, and security of the surrounding states and the world at large due to the enormous amount of refugees fleeing the country. This instability has been most obvious in the development and spread of various armed militias and terrorist groups in Syria and in neighboring countries. The conflict has created a major power vacuum in many parts of Syria, leaving control of the area ripe for the picking.

While many analysts and experts on the region predicted increasing chaos as the violence continued,[2] inaction on the part of the international community allowed for foreign fighters from terrorist groups to set up shop and begin planning attacks against the Assad regime. This was one of a few reasons that Russia and China--both U.N. Security Council members with veto powers and often allied with Syria--vehemently disagreed with Western interference in the civil war. As conditions continued to deteriorate, many more armed groups joined the fight. These different militias and terrorist groups often claim to have the support of the locals in whose city they occupy in their efforts against the Syrian government forces. The allegiances among these groups have changed often and their tactics have varied as they have taken on the Syrian Army and, at times, each other.

Chapter 2: The Foundations of the Al-Nusra Front

Al-Qaeda, or "The Base" in Arabic, is one of the most famous and notorious of all modern terrorist groups. Of course, Al-Qaeda's notoriety skyrocketed after the devastating terrorist attacks on September 11, 2001 in New York, Pennsylvania, and Virginia, killing nearly 3,000 people in one day and injuring many more.[3] Moreover, Al-Qaeda's influence on Islamic jihadist movements and ideology cannot be understated: their development of guides for spreading propaganda, magazines, weapons training, black market activities, and other illegal connections was and still is very widespread and strong. They have been associated with various terrorist groups around the world and have developed regional branches for their activities in Africa, the Middle East and South Asia. While the ultimate goal of establishing and spreading an Islamic caliphate has always been the same, Al-Qaeda and most of their local affiliates have developed the ability to target political and social dynamics in their host countries in attempts to build support for their terrorist activities, whether through recruitment efforts against the regime they are fighting or in the aftermath of their terrorist attacks. Terrorism, at the heart of the matter, is about provoking extreme action on the part of governments in response to attacks against civilians or public places. The idea is to provoke such a large action on the part of a government

[2] International Crisis Group. (2011, November 3). *Syria's Tipping Point*. Retrieved from International Crisis Group: https://www.crisisgroup.org/middle-east-north-africa/eastern-mediterranean/syria/syria-s-tipping-poin
[3] Global Security. (2016, July 8). *Al-Qaida/Al-Qaeda (The Base)*. Retrieved from Global Security: http://www.globalsecurity.org/military/world/para/al-qaida.htm

that civilian casualties are massive. When this happens, Al-Qaeda can capitalize upon the anger and sadness of the local population, either through increased recruitment or increased supporters among the civilians.

Al-Qaeda in Iraq (AQI) was established in 2004 following the U.S. invasion of Iraq.[4] During the turmoil of the war against the regime of Saddam Hussein, Sunni militant groups joined the fight and organized armed resistance through an insurgency in the country. As the war waxed and waned over the years, Al-Qaeda took responsibility for much destruction and numerous vicious attacks against civilians, soldiers, and religious sites throughout the country. While Al-Qaeda has undergone a few iterations over the past 10 years and experienced huge blows to their top leadership - most notably the killings of Osama bin Laden and Abu Mu'sab Al-Zarqawi (who died in a U.S. airstrike in 2006) - the group's ability to remain resilient has been one of its many defining features.[5] It is nearly impossible to determine how many militants are part of Al-Qaeda because of its decentralized structure and due to members of other jihadist groups' simultaneously cooperating with each other in operations across battlefields.

Zarqawi

Perhaps just as importantly today, this decentralization has also led to the development of other

---

[4] Encyclopaedia Britannica. (2015, October 27). *Al-Qaeda in Iraq (AQI)*. Retrieved from Encyclopaedia Britannica: https://www.britannica.com/topic/Al-Qaeda-in-Iraq
[5] Ibid

groups inspired by Al-Qaeda's jihadist ideology around the world, such as Boko Haram in Nigeria. This inspiration for independent operations has come to define groups such as the Islamic State (ISIL) and Ansar Al-Sharia, who had seemingly not received direct instruction from any kind of central leadership but carried out terrorist attacks inspired by the movement more generally. [6]

Localized development of terror cells creates a very peculiar and difficult situation for states attempting to counter terrorism and violent extremism. Groups such as Jabhat Al-Nusra do not merely live among populations in the states in which they operate; they are actively recruiting and developing connections and trying to build trust, a very similar model that Hezbollah in Lebanon has taken on over the past 35 years. These groups understand that long-term "success" can only be defined by the willingness of the population to not only surrender to the violent tactics the groups enact, but also feel sympathy and support for those "martyred" by the cause.

ISIL has taken a very different path, defined by its severe brutality and relentlessness to force populations in Syria and Iraq to submit to their control. Some analysts believe, however, that ISIL is not as much of a threat as groups like Jabhat Al-Nusra. According to the Institute for the Study of War: "Jabhat al Nusra draws strength from its intertwinement with Syrian Sunni opposition groups. The slow pace of U.S. strategy and its exclusive prioritization of ISIS are facilitating Jabhat al Nusra's deeper entrenchment within the opposition...Identifying means of separating Jabhat al Nusra from the opposition in order to destroy it is the most difficult intellectual task in developing a strategy for Syria..." [7]

When the Arab Spring began in 2011 and chaos ensued in Syria, AQI seized upon the opportunity and sent operatives across the Iraq-Syria border. This was commanded by Abu Bakr al-Baghdadi, a top leader in AQI at that time and the figure that would go on to found and lead ISIL. [8] Abu Muhammad Al-Julani was among this group and took the lead in developing Jabhat Al-Nusra in Syria. Their goal was to garner support among fearful, Sunni Syrians while attempting to consolidate all militant groups in the area under their banner. During this time, Al-Nusra developed its cell inside Syria and recruited among the Syrian population. They, in effect, laid the ground work for a counter operation against the Assad regime.

---

[6] Bajoria, J. a. (2012, June 6). *Backgrounder: Al-Qaeda (a.k.a. al-Qaida, al-Qa'ida)*. Retrieved from Council on Foreign Relations: http://www.cfr.org/terrorist-organizations-and-networks/al-qaeda-k-al-qaida-al-qaida/p9126

[7] Cafarella, J. H. (2016, February). *U.S. GRAND STRATEGY: Destroying ISIS and Al-Qaeda, Report Three.* Retrieved from Institute for the Study of War: http://www.understandingwar.org/sites/default/files/PLANEX%20Report%203%20FINAL.pdf
[8] Lister, C. R. (2016, July). *Profiling Jabhat Al-Nusra.* Retrieved from Brookings Institution: https://www.brookings.edu/wp-content/uploads/2016/07/iwr_20160728_profiling_nusra.pdf

Al-Baghdadi

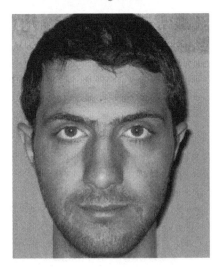

Al-Julani

During the mid-2000s, Al-Qaeda experienced a rise and fall of its various occupied territories around Iraq. Throughout this time period, Al-Qaeda leadership declared the establishment of the Islamic State of Iraq (ISI) which included many cities and provinces, such as Anbar and Baghdad. [9] Their control over these areas around Iraq changed frequently over time depending on the actions of the U.S.-led coalition involvement in Iraq and their various surges. ISI/Al-Qaeda ramped up their attacks around Iraq in 2008 and 2009 and when the civil war in Syria broke out in 2011, this was a prime opportunity for the group to spread its propaganda and operations to another state dealing with the chaos left by an ongoing war.

When Abu Muhammad Al-Julani and other top leaders came to Syria, they aimed to create chaos and thereby establish a space "receptive" to their propaganda and actions. These attacks utilize "urban-rural warfare" which focuses on taking over rural periphery locals while slowly flowing into urban city centers.[10] This tactic has led to the capture and hold of Idlib in the northwest and Deir Al-Zour in the eastern part of Syria.

In 2013 and 2014, the term "Khorasan Group" became more prominent in the media. The term, most likely coined by the U.S., referred to a group of about 50 core leaders in Al-Qaeda primarily from operations in Afghanistan and Pakistan. [11] According to U.S. intelligence reports, this group was sent by Al-Qaeda central leadership to Syria to further recruit and develop a network of fighters and plan attacks against countries from Syria, primarily those thought to be allied with Western states. Many of the individuals in the group were well-acquainted with Bin Laden and worked with him and his organization in past operations, like the terrorist attacks of September 11, 2001. The Khorasan Group worked to continue to lay the foundation for Jabhat Al-Nusra. This group claims to operate in support of the people of Syria against the regime of Bashar Assad and Western encroachment in the civil war.

When Abu Muhammad Al-Julani and his group were sent to Syria in 2011, their mission was to develop operations quickly and effectively throughout the country, ideally leading the linking of several disparate militias and terrorist groups already active in the area. According to the Quilliam Foundation, their goals were 5-fold:

1. to establish a group including many existing jihadists, linking them together into one coherent entity
2. to reinforce and strengthen the consciousness of the Islamist nature of the conflict

[9] Roggio, B. (2006, October 16). *The Rump Islamic Emirate of Iraq*. Retrieved from The Long War Journal: http://www.longwarjournal.org/archives/2006/10/the_rump_islamic_emi.php# (Roggio, 2006)
[10] Benotman, N. a. (n.d.). *Jabhat Al-Nusra: A Strategic Briefing*. Retrieved from Quilliam Foundation: https://web.archive.org/web/20150328080133/http://www.quilliamfoundation.org/wp/wp-content/uploads/publications/free/jabhat-al-nusra-a-strategic-briefing.pdf
[11] BBC News. (2014, September 24). *What is the Khorasan Group?* Retrieved from BBC New: http://www.bbc.com/news/world-middle-east-29350271

3.   to build military capacity for the group, seizing opportunities to collect weapons and train recruits, and to create safe havens by controlling physical places upon which to exercise their power.
4.   to create an Islamist state in Syria
5.   to establish a 'Caliphate' in Bilad al-Sham (the Levant) [12]

The group is made up of veteran jihadists from the area who are primarily Syrian but also from outside Syria that have fought in other jihadist ventures with Al-Qaeda, which already sets them apart from the other seemingly rag-tag group of revolutionaries like the Free Syrian Army. For all intents and purposes, AQI/ISI funded Jabhat Al-Nusra's activities in Syria, particularly by building on their previously utilized funding stream of captured oil fields and ransoms from kidnappings. Al-Nusra also supports itself through the weapons it is able to take following battles and with its connections with other militant groups in the country. It has not been uncommon to see Al-Nusra on the battlefield with other groups fighting alongside each other against the Syrian army. There are also reports of the group fighting these very same militants as well, which signifies a larger strategic issue for Al-Nusra's operations in Syria. As much as it needs to ally with the other groups, it cannot risk being subsumed.

Chapter 3: Ideology and Tactics

Like most Islamic Sunni jihadist organizations, Jabhat Al-Nusra's ultimate goal is to develop a caliphate on Earth, based on their idealized understanding of how life after the Prophet Muhammad was intended to be led and organized. Al-Nusra's ideology is Salafi--a very conservative form of Islam whose development and prominence in the Islamic world spread during the 19th century. Essentially, Salafists envision a world entirely modeled after the time of the Prophet, where strict adherence to religious law and custom are valued above innovation and convergence with modernity. This world vision sees the time of the Prophet as the most perfect and a time to be desired and emulated.

Al-Nusra is certainly not the first group to attempt to control a society by religious law; in fact, some of their purported supporters (like Qatar) already control society with conservative notions of religious law. The difference, however, is that Al-Nusra and other groups often use extreme violence in their efforts to command the society to behave in a particular way. Reports coming out of ISIL-controlled territory indicate large-scale executions, beheadings, amputations, and other extreme brutality enacted against civilians. In the videos produced by ISIL showing these actions, ISIL fighters indicate the "crime" committed by the civilian in religious terms and will connect the punishment back to Islam using their own interpretation of the religion. These fighters are not religious leaders or scholars by any means, but they have perfected the art of jihadism, essentially drawing connections between parts of the Qu'ran and Hadith (the sayings

---

[12] Benotman, N. a. (n.d.). *Jabhat Al-Nusra: A Strategic Briefing.* Retrieved from Quilliam Foundation: https://web.archive.org/web/20150328080133/http://www.quilliamfoundation.org/wp/wp-content/uploads/publications/free/jabhat-al-nusra-a-strategic-briefing.pdf

and actions of the Prophet Muhammad) dictating punishment without any regard for contexts and historical understandings.

While both Jabhat Al-Nusra and ISIL have their roots in Al-Qaeda's jihadist ideology and have recruited fighters from Al-Qaeda's ranks for their respective fights and territories, their leaders have fought over the group's direction and tactics. Both Al-Nusra and ISIL's leaders--Abu Muhammad Al-Julani and Abu Bakr Al-Baghdadi, respectively--have their origins among Al-Qaeda's ranks, and in fact, Al-Baghdadi was the leader of Al-Qaeda in Iraq (AQI) and responsible for sending fighters into Syria to develop Jabhat Al-Nusra. While Al-Julani was taking orders from Al-Baghdadi's leadership team in developing Al-Nusra's operations in Syria, a disagreement among those at the top in Al-Qaeda was taking place. Ayman Al-Zawahiri, the current leader of Al-Qaeda and long-time #2 behind Bin Laden, had encouraged Al-Baghdadi to develop operations in Iraq, but Al-Baghdad's desire for control eventually led to a breakaway from Al-Qaeda and the development of ISIL.[13]

Zawahiri

In order for Al-Baghdadi to further solidify his power in the region as ISIL developed, he made

[13] Byman, D. L. (2015, February 24). *ISIS vs. Al Qaeda: Jihadism's global civil war*. Retrieved from Brookings Institution: https://www.brookings.edu/articles/isis-vs-al-qaeda-jihadisms-global-civil-war/

a statement in 2013 indicating that Jabhat Al-Nusra was actually a splinter group of ISIL and operated at their request and under his direction. In response, Abu Muhammad Al-Julani responded that while they had worked with ISIS and received considerable support (particularly when ISIS was still linked with Al-Qaeda), their ultimate loyalty was with Al-Qaeda and Al-Zawahiri.[14] These statements led to many responses among other jihadist groups and Al-Qaeda itself declaring allegiance with one side or the other. According to Mary Habeck, "The early dispute between Jabhat al-Nusra and ISIS was, then, about *power*: who would swear bay'a to whom and, therefore, which commander was subordinate and which was in charge. It was also about which commander and group would have a closer relationship with Al-Qaeda's leadership, showing how much the favor of Al-Qaeda was prized."[15] As the conflict further inflamed relations among the groups and ISIS took more territory and grew in strength throughout 2013 and 2014, Al-Qaeda formally denounced ISIS' behavior due to its extremely violent approaches to subduing populations (including indiscriminate killing of Muslims) in the areas that it controlled which it considered against Islamic law.

The split and differentiation between ISIS and Al-Qaeda affiliated groups like Jabhat Al-Nusra eventually began to center around a different understanding of ideology and tactics used to create and maintain the Islamic caliphates. Al-Qaeda has generally focused on the West and specifically on the United States as its primary enemy but has understood that in order to continue to be relevant in the context of the post-Arab Spring uprisings, a shift in focus on particular Arab regimes must become a priority. In Iraq, ISIL has focused on bringing down the Iraqi government and, just as its affiliated groups throughout the region, on various Arab and primarily secular regimes such as in Egypt, Tunisia, and Libya while also encouraging lone wolf attacks throughout the West. Jabhat Al-Nusra has also, at Al-Qaeda's command, focused on bringing down Bashar Assad's regime but, as mentioned above, has not strayed away from the "far enemy" idea that the U.S. is responsible for the ills of the Muslim world, as espoused by Al-Qaeda.[16]

Just as with other militant groups in and around Syria, Al-Nusra has tried to strike a balance between collaboration and control of the local population. As much as it may agree with ISIL's ideology and many of its tactics, it does not want to be controlled by a group much larger and, seemingly, more powerful than itself, especially since ISIL has decided to strike out on its own and commit many of the same mistakes that Al-Qaeda committed in the past, such as extremely harsh behavior toward civilians and indiscriminate killing. Many experts believe that Al-Nusra is "playing the long game"[17] when it comes to jihadist movements in the region. This is because

[14] Habeck, M. (2014, June 27). *Assessing the ISIS - Al-Qaeda Split: The Origins of the Dispute.* Retrieved from Insite Blog on Terrorism & Extremism: http://news.siteintelgroup.com/blog/index.php/categories/jihad/entry/193-assessing-the-isis-al-qaeda-split-the-origins-of-the-dispute-1
[15] Ibid
[16] Byman, D. L. (2015, February 24). *ISIS vs. Al Qaeda: Jihadism's global civil war.* Retrieved from Brookings Institution: https://www.brookings.edu/articles/isis-vs-al-qaeda-jihadisms-global-civil-war/
[17] Schatz, B. (2016, August 5). *Meet the Terrorist Group Playing the Long Game in Syria.* Retrieved from MotherJones: http://www.motherjones.com/politics/2016/08/syria-al-qaeda-nusra-battle-aleppo

they have yet to carry out an all-out assault against civilians and different militant groups in the area like ISIL continues to do in its territory. Al-Nusra operates under the assumption that ISIL will burn out as it continues to gain much of the international community's focus and attention. Al-Nusra on the other hand, is operating a little under the radar as it cultivates relationships among the Syrian population.

Thus, while Al-Nusra most definitely interprets religious texts in a similar way and makes those connections in terms of controlling the society they want to develop, their approach has been less harsh and brutal than ISIL's methods. They are intent on developing institutions in order to solidify their rule and commanded behavior. To this end, Jabhat Al-Nusra has developed councils (shuras) and courts to administer religious law (shari'a) throughout the areas they control in Syria. According to the Quilliam Foundation, "They and other rebel groups are experiencing a lack of religious scholars to lead prayers and spread their religious message, leading to call for imams to come to Syria from abroad."[18] These imams advise the military leaders and work to resolve disputes in the communities while enacting "God's laws on earth."

As noted earlier, localized cells of Al-Qaeda have shifted their strategy, for the most part, on developing trust and legitimacy among the communities where they launch attacks against the regimes they fight against. Over the past 4 years, Jabhat Al-Nusra has operated in cities and towns on Syria's eastern border with Iraq and around the western borders with Lebanon and Turkey. According to Middle East Institute analyst Charles Lister, "[Jabhat Al-Nusra] has played a methodically implemented long game in Syria, focused on attaining a position of military and social influence and, crucially, establishing a relationship of interdependence with Syria's opposition."[19] Their tactics have been less violent and extreme, according to Lister, "in order to present a friendly face to local communities." This emphasis on building legitimacy continues to impact their operations throughout the country. By emphasizing their intent to support "Syria," they are trying to dispel any idea that they are a foreign group, which has in fact led to disagreement among leadership in Al-Nusra and Al-Qaeda in Iraq.

In order to develop and foster this support, Jabhat Al-Nusra has taken a page right of Hezbollah's book and set up a "Relief Department" focused on distributing goods to the population where they reside.[20] As part of their tactics, Al-Nusra records and distributes videos of this "good behavior," such as distributing food, providing health care, and delivering other services.[21] These activities attempt to further solidify not only the local community's desired

---

[18] Ibid

[19] Schatz, B. (2016, August 5). *Meet the Terrorist Group Playing the Long Game in Syria.* Retrieved from MotherJones: http://www.motherjones.com/politics/2016/08/syria-al-qaeda-nusra-battle-aleppo

[20] Benotman, N. a. (n.d.). *Jabhat Al-Nusra: A Strategic Briefing.* Retrieved from Quilliam Foundation: https://web.archive.org/web/20150328080133/http://www.quilliamfoundation.org/wp/wp-content/uploads/publications/free/jabhat-al-nusra-a-strategic-briefing.pdf

[21] Gartenstein-Ross, D. a. (2013, August 22). *How Syria's Jihadists Win Friends and Influence People.* Retrieved from The Atlantic: http://www.theatlantic.com/international/archive/2013/08/how-syrias-jihadists-win-friends-and-influence-people/278942

perception change toward Al-Nusra, but also increases reliance on the group. On occasions where a city is under siege, goods and services are clearly not going to come from the Syrian government. This is where Jabhat Al-Nusra steps in and begins to develop those relationships with the local community. This strategic positioning helps their public image tremendously.

Such behavior is very common among jihadist and political groups throughout the Middle East, such as the aforementioned Hezbollah in Lebanon and the Muslim Brotherhood in Egypt. When governments are unable or refuse to provide services to poorer communities or those in the periphery of the country, a gap is filled by these groups hoping to sway opinion in their favor. In some cases, the services provided, such as medical care, are better than those provided by the government.[22] This complex reality poses a very unique challenge to not only counter-terrorism but also countering violent extremism in a larger way. It is not enough to destroy a terrorist group and prevent recruitment; the very root causes of people joining extremist groups, such as gaps in services and lack of employment, must be addressed as well to lead to long term development.

When it comes to imposing and administering religion in its captured territories, Al-Nusra is taking a different approach than ISIL. Reports from the field indicate that while Al-Nusra most definitely calls people to religion and desires to enforce religion on the area, their tactics change when they encounter resistance. In 2015, there was a report of Al-Nusra fighters shooting Druze in Idlib purportedly because they supported Bashar Assad and, in other instances, they forced Druze to destroy their shrines and to abide by shari'a law.[23] While these actions are obviously repressive and harsh, Al-Nusra tries to make a distinction between itself and the way ISIL treats minorities in its territory, like Christians and Yazidis (e.g., completely slaughter). The leader of Jabhat Al-Nusra, Abu Muhammad Al-Julani, even published a video in 2015 stating that their enemies were not the West, but Bashar Assad.[24]

When people look back and analyze the Arab Spring revolutions during late 2010 and 2011, Twitter and Facebook immediately come to mind as the launch pads where these uprisings appeared to organize. Protesters organized, debated, and reported from the field what was happening as they attempted to overturn their governments and work toward real change in the region. In most cases, as the world has come to know, the ultimate reality of social, democratic and regime change has not been completely realized (and in some cases, has only worsened), but Twitter and Facebook are still the primary medium for exchanging information and reporting on events among activists, civil society leaders and journalists.

---

[22] Farag, N. (2014). *Between Piety and Politics: Social Services and the Muslim Brotherhood.* Retrieved from Frontline - PBS: http://www.pbs.org/wgbh/pages/frontline/revolution-in-cairo/inside-muslim-brotherhood/piety-and-politics.html
[23] yalibnan. (2015, March 19). *Al Qaeda forces Druze of Idlib Syria to destory their shrines and convert.* Retrieved from YaLibnan: http://yalibnan.com/2015/03/19/al-qaeda-forces-druze-of-idlib-syria-to-destroy-their-shrines-and-convert
[24] Fanack - Chronicle. (2015, July 1). *Jabhat Al-Nusra Tries to Look Like a Moderate Terrorist Group.* Retrieved from Fanack - Chronicle of the Middle East & North Africa: https://chronicle.fanack.com/specials/extremism/jabhat-al-nusra-tries-to-look-a-moderate-terrorist-group/

This has been nowhere near as obvious as in Syria. Activists and civilians have reported the human rights abuses of Assad's military through quick, short tweets and relevant hashtags, which have allowed journalists, policymakers and analysts to keep track of what is happening on the ground, especially since it is too dangerous for the average journalist and the Internet connection has been cut in many areas.

Naturally, the immensely successful ability of Twitter to pass this information on quickly and widely did not go unnoticed by jihadist groups like Jabhat Al-Nusra. According to analysts Nico Prucha and Ali Fisher, "Jihadists...soon adapted that content and the platform for their own propaganda purposes. By rebranding and reframing the content created by civil society activists, jihadists used these grievances to support a key jihadist theme: the obligation to defend and protect the Sunni population in Syria." [25] This grievance is very similar in nature to those used by other jihadist groups around the world: that a particular Muslim population is being targeted because of their religious affiliation and therefore, they are in need of protection.

This idea has helped to shaped the Syrian Civil War narrative into a religious war when, for the most part, it did not start that way. While Assad is an Alawi Muslim (a type of Shi'ite) and has received support from Iran, he has ruled his country in a secular way under the control of the Ba'athist party, much like Saddam Hussein in Iraq. The Ba'athists are a secular, socialist party actually started by Michel Aflaq, a Syrian Greek Orthodox Christian. Also much like in Iraq, the victim narrative was turned on its head and the conflict has regressed into religious terminology and framing in order to serve the interests of warring parties. It is not surprising then that a majority of Syrian Christians actually support Assad's government out of fear that Islamism in the region will lead to complete Sunni dominance imposing religious law like in ISIL-controlled territory.

---

[25] Prucha, N. a. (2013, June 25). *Tweeting for the Caliphate: Twitter as the New Frontier for Jihadist Propaganda*. Retrieved from Combating Terrorist Center at West Point: https://www.ctc.usma.edu/posts/tweeting-for-the-caliphate-twitter-as-the-new-frontier-for-jihadist-propaganda

Aflaq

Some of Jabhat Al-Nusra's top figures are propagandists responsible for developing materials for use to spread through social media, particularly through Twitter. During the summer of 2014, the world became very aware of ISIL's activities on Twitter, from the cute and shareable pictures of jihadists holding kittens to the pictures of black-cloaked men riding jeeps holding guns in the air. Analysts were quick to spot trends in the spread of propaganda materials through Twitter, Facebook and YouTube. Many of these propaganda videos attempting to recruit or spread the messages of ISIL were notable due to their sophistication in video editing and the rather unique or "Western" manner in which the group was able to push out the materials online. The messages of ISIL centered on the idea of dissatisfaction among Muslim populations in the West, particularly with youth who felt as though they were not part of the community that they were living in. In addition to this, ISIL has taken the narrative among some Westerners that Islam, Arabs, or those who have originated in the Middle East cannot fit into Western culture since it is heavily influenced by Judeo-Christian values. These extremely complex and harsh sentiments are the cornerstone of ISIL's mission and recruitment efforts toward Western audience. The propaganda showing ISIL's military victories, life in their territory, and messages for their enemies are fuel for their online battlefield aimed at recruiting fighters and intimidating the U.S. led coalition.

Jabhat Al-Nusra's online audience is not so much Western-focused as it is focused on Syria, their surrounding neighbors, and Al-Qaeda supporters. For while ISIL is trying to gain and maintain legitimacy in the world-at-large for their mission to create a caliphate in Iraq and Syria, Jabhat Al-Nusra has zeroed in on the audience it needs to build legitimacy and support for its war against Assad. As of 2015, it was estimated that Internet penetration in Syria was about 28% and that about 5% of the population actually used the Internet.[26] Despite this seemingly low reach to Syrians themselves, Twitter's ability to disseminate information through hashtags has helped disseminate Al-Nusra's information widely. This also helps Al-Nusra to maintain a semblance of legitimacy among would-be allies and enemies.

There are several reports among data analysts who look at social media engagement rates that indicate the likes and re-tweeting of Twitter materials among Al-Nusra, particularly those using the hashtag #جبهة_النصرة (Jabhat Al-Nusra in Arabic). In many cases, the tweets have embedded links to YouTube showing martyrdom videos of Al-Nusra fighters and scenes from battles on the field against Syrian government forces. Some of the other most popular and most viewed videos focus on the behavior of Al-Nusra members toward the civilians in the town or city that they operate, such as protecting civilians from gunfire and explosions while also targeting soldiers they claim are those supporters of Bashar Assad's government. The framing of the content is incredibly important, again, because of its intended purpose of showing its viewers how Al-Nusra's main intent is to protect Syrian Sunni Muslims against the Assad government. The more that the group can film their actions and frame them in this manner, the more the group is able to work on developing legitimacy among the population.

The manner in which Jabhat Al-Nusra spreads its propaganda is more structured than that of ISIL. There have been several Western government attempts over the last few years to slow or completely delete and remove ISIL-created content on social media platforms. This has led to ISIL supporters and leaders having a disparate network of accounts simultaneously created and banned across Twitter. This has also been aided by the fact that ISIL is always in the news and the primary concern for most initiatives to counter violent extremism.

Jabhat Al-Nusra, on the other hand, has been flying under the radar since 2012. According to the site Vox, "Nusra has 10 official Twitter accounts through which it spreads its propaganda. Nusra's propaganda network on Twitter is split between 1 main central account and 9 other secondary accounts. The 9 secondary accounts post various kinds of propaganda from different regions in Syria." [27] The central account and media department of the group, Al-Manarat Al-

[26] Internet World Stats. (2015, November). *Internet Usage in the Middle East.* Retrieved from Internet World Stats. http://www.Internetworldstats.com/stats5.htm

[27] *How Jabhat Al Nusra Uses Twitter to Spread Propaganda.* (2016, May 4). Retrieved from VOX Pol: http://www.voxpol.eu/how-jabhat-al-nusra-uses-twitter-to-spread-propaganda/

Bayda, translated as "The White Minaret" in Arabic, is noted for looking very much like a news organization with branded logos, colors, and designs. [28] In order to continue to produce their content over these social media platforms, Al-Nusra has become skilled at using different hashtags to link their tweets and connect them to their supporters. VOX further proposes that Al-Nusra uses previously created Twitter accounts when their newer ones are banned, which helps them to develop ads and promote their propaganda videos using the Twitter Ads program. For those that are unable to access the Internet, they have developed CDs full of propaganda materials to distribute throughout the country.[29]

Thus, while this important fact is overlooked, the truth is that Jabhat Al-Nusra fights many of its battles online. It has to contend not only with ISIL and social media platforms' rules and regulations, but also with developing its particular jihadist content in a way to serve its purpose of promoting legitimacy among their supporters and would-be followers in and around Syria. Indeed, Al-Nusra's ability to combine their tech-savvy content promotion schemes while learning from ISIL's mistakes has helped them to stay alive and strong on Twitter and YouTube. As of now, Al-Nusra's Twitter activity analyzed indicates there are over 12,000 connections and 7,000 accounts using the Arabic hashtag #جبهة_النصرة.[30] Their content mixes videos of Nusra fighters "good deeds" done for Syrian civilians with their battleground efforts, offering an alternative to ISIL's brutal tactics.

Chapter 4: Jabhat Al-Nusra's Battlefields

The complex situation surrounding the development of the Syrian Civil War and its primary opponents provides a unique space for Jabhat Al-Nusra. Many Western governments felt as though they were between a rock and a hard place when it came to supporting protesters throughout the region during the wave of protests during the Arab Spring; they wanted to support the protesters in hopes that it would eventually lead to the toppling of dictators in the region who, in most cases, were the primary roadblock to a series of developmental initiatives such as the institutionalization of democracy, but at the same time, those very same dictators had become strong allies bent on preventing the well-organized Islamist groups from taking hold of government institutions (these groups, of course, were primarily anti-Western oriented in their militant actions).

The case of Syria was essentially the same, but Bashar Assad's unique relationship with Iran and Russia made things particularly thorny for the United States and its allies. Russia's continual blocking of United Nations resolutions to condemn and act against the Syrian regime were

---

[28] Ibid

[29] Benotman, N. a. (n.d.). *Jabhat Al-Nusra: A Strategic Briefing.* Retrieved from Quilliam Foundation: https://web.archive.org/web/20150328080133/http://www.quilliamfoundation.org/wp/wp-content/uploads/publications/free/jabhat-al-nusra-a-strategic-briefing.pdf

[30] Barna, C. (2014). The Road to Jihad in Syria: Using SOCMINT to Counter the Radicalization of Muslim Youth in Romania. In M. Lombardi, E. Ragab, V. Chin, Y. Dandurand, V. de Divitiis, & A. Burato, *Countering Radicalisation and Youth Extremism Among Youth to Prevent Terrorism.* Milan: IOS Press

justified by claiming Assad's regime was defending itself against terrorists, the very same claim Bashar himself gave in many of his public addresses during the war. How could the West claim to support rebels in Syria when the rebels' tactics included what they themselves counted as terrorism? And with Russian anger and disapproval lurking not far from the conflict, how could the West intervene without awaking the Russian Bear?

This indecisiveness in the conflict worked in the jihadists' favor. While the world now is intimately familiar with ISIL's rise to notoriety in Iraq and Syria due to the vacuum that opened up in both countries, Jabhat Al-Nusra's activity has not been much of a central focus during this time. ISIL's ability to attract media attention for their beheadings, mass killings, and brutal repression of minorities has worked in Al-Nusra's favor. Since Al-Nusra's inception in early 2012, they have cooperated with the many militias on the ground in Syria against the Assad regime. Their cooperation has, as aforementioned, led to an increase in recruitment as well as support among civilians.

According to Lina Khatib of *Syria Deeply*, Al-Nusra has also won favor because it is seen as a group that has taken on corruption in the aftermath of the war. [31] A few of the militant groups on the ground have suffered from infighting and the development of warlords around the country. Al-Nusra, on the other hand, has worked to integrate these groups ostensibly for the greater good of Syria. The groups that Al-Nusra has not attempted to integrate, however, it has challenged and battled, such as the Syrian Revolutionaries Front and the Hazm Movement. According to Khatib, Al-Nusra has claimed that it fought these groups due to corruption and affiliation with the United States, but it is most likely due to these groups posing a challenge to Al-Nusra's legitimacy. "Through alliances with certain groups, acquisitions and defeat of others, Jabhat Al Nusra aims to strengthen its footprint and widen its influence in the north, and present itself as the primary force fighting the Assad regime on the ground." [32] When the U.S. carries out airstrikes against Al-Nusra, this only further emboldens their followers.

While it is unlikely that Jabhat Al-Nusra will ever be able to militarily overcome the Syrian government's forces, they are aiming to be a viable option for Sunnis when the war finally comes to an end, much like Hezbollah has done for Shiites following the Lebanese Civil War in the early 1990s. If the recent experiences of Tunisia and Egypt following the Arab Spring revolutions are any indication of the popularity of Islamist groups as an alternative to brutal dictatorships, then Jabhat Al-Nusra may very well end up being a viable option for the beleaguered Syrian population. The Freedom and Justice Party in Egypt and Ennahda in Tunisia were very much involved in politics and even led their countries' governments in the aftermath of the Arab Spring protests. Their ability to come to prominence quickly following the fall of Hosni Mubarak in Egypt and Zine Al-Abedine Bin Ali in Tunisia was most likely because these

---

[31] Montgomery, K. (2015, April 13). *Jabhat Al Nusra: A Game Change in Syria.* Retrieved from World Policy Blog: http://www.worldpolicy.org/blog/2015/04/13/jabhat-al-nusra-game-changer-syri

[32] Ibid

groups had developed a solid support base and were the most organized political groups, thereby filling a void leading up to the first ever democratic elections in these countries. Though these groups eventually ended up facing conflict and societal pushback in various ways, their effects are still very much felt in Egypt and Tunisia. The Muslim Brotherhood from whence both political groups emerged did a very good job of reaching out and providing services on the ground when the government often could not or would not, thereby shaping the perceptions and feelings of local populations toward the group. In the same vein, Jabhat Al-Nusra is providing these kinds of services while showing their might where it is most needed--on the battlefield-- while attempting to mould the Syrian Sunni imagination to what "could be" for the future of their country when the war finally comes to its inevitable conclusion.

Since Jabhat Al-Nusra's main *modus operandi* centers around the distinction they wish to make with ISIL and other militant groups in the region, when Al-Nusra comes to town, they are not looking to violently force conversion among the civilians or slaughter them in the areas they take over, at least not initially. On the contrary, they are hoping to "win hearts and minds" by offering services, protection and a new vision for Syria's future. Al-Nusra is attempting to make life for civilians in their occupied territories as close to it was before the civil war began as possible while slowly, but surely, injecting their particular brand of Salafi Islamism into the local society. This is without a doubt a reflection of their roots in Al-Qaeda's ideology and an apparent learning of its past mistakes when trying to take over and win the support of groups in their occupied territories.

When Jabhat Al-Nusra first takes over a location, it does not immediately oust any current leaders or groups in charge of the area. Instead, it generally tries to work together to control and administer the town or city over a period of time--unless it has faced fierce opposition, such as in Druze majority areas. When Al-Nusra has garnered enough support among the population, only then will it take on any opposition remaining. "This often means beginning with *da'wa*, or proselytization, which al-Nusra frequently deploys through its publications, public events, and everyday interactions with non-members. It often launches a string of extensive *da'wa* campaigns, led by local and foreign clerics and fighters. These campaigns double as recruitment events and as platforms to promote their political project."[33]

By proselytizing, they are trying to convince the local population that if and when Bashar Assad's government falls, the only alternative must be an Islamic-run state, or caliphate. The neighborhoods campaigns aimed at recruiting also offer this vision of what Al-Nusra believes Syria could be in the region--essentially, Al-Qaeda's state. The more Al-Nusra conflates Assad's regime with chaos while simultaneously offering an alternative of an Islamic state led by jihad, the more entrenched they become in the local community.

---

[33] Abbas, Y. (2016, May 10). *How Al-Qaeda is Winning in Syria*. Retrieved from War on the Rocks: http://warontherocks.com/2016/05/how-al-qaeda-is-winning-in-syria

This process of indoctrination among the local population happens at many levels in the society. When it comes to the children, Al-Nusra has set up academies aimed at recruiting the next generation of jihadists to fight in its army. Documentarian Medyan Dairieh was able to gain exclusive access to Al-Nusra's top leadership back in 2015 and filmed on location in parts of Syria. In this documentary produced by VICE News, Dairieh filmed and interviewed young boys taking part in Al-Nusra's jihadist academies. These young boys came from around Syria and there was even one young student who came all the way from Uzbekistan. The academy focused on teaching Arabic, religious education, and physical fitness in order to train the next generation of fighters.[34] Throughout the documentary, viewers can see instances of the boys chanting and singing songs reveling in the jihad and the wars to come. This is in juxtaposition to what is seen with the fighters on the field, who also start their day with such songs and oaths to follow Osama Bin Laden's footsteps to fight the United States and the Jews. Interestingly, while these fighters discuss the U.S. and its allies as their main source of contention, it is repeated that the main enemy at this time is actually Bashar Assad and, at times, the Lebanese Army in the south. This is indicative of Al-Qaeda's older ideology focused on destruction of the West in general and the U.S. more specifically. As much as Al-Nusra desires to infiltrate into Syrian society by directing their attacks toward the Syrian regime, their core ideology has not changed and will remain pivoting around the desire to develop a larger, global Islamic caliphate wherein they view the United States as their primary obstacle in doing so. Their leader Abu Muhammad Al-Julani even went so far as to claim he had no animosity toward the West unless they interfere in his operations against the Syrian regime.[35]

While Al-Nusra presents a particular image to the world of a "kinder, gentler terrorist group," this has not been the experience of everyone living under their rule. In Idlib province in northwestern Syria, some civilians have reported very harsh living conditions. After the group took control, many people who Al-Nusra accused of being Bashar Assad supporters or government employees were imprisoned or executed, and the group immediately began changing practices in the local community. One woman reported that they removed science and history classes from schools and changed the focus to Islamic education. She discussed how "religious police" walked the streets to make sure women and men were dressed appropriately.[36]

Obviously, people can definitely draw parallels with the activities of ISIL in Iraq and Syria. In order for these extremist groups to develop the type of society they want--which they claim is modeled after the time of the Prophet Muhammad--they feel that their only option is to make a particular action, dress or behavior mandatory among the local population. This is, of course, a type of rule and control. Al-Nusra, ISIL and other such groups control their population under

[34] Daireh, M. (2015, November 11). *Inside the Battle: Al Nusra-Al Qaeda in Syria*. Retrieved from VICE News: https://news.vice.com/video/inside-the-battle-al-nusra-al-qaeda-in-syria

[35] BBC News. (2015, May 28). *Al-Qaeda 'orders Syria's Al-Nusra Front not to attack West'*. Retrieved from BBC News: http://www.bbc.com/news/world-middle-east-32913509

[36] Hall, R. a. (2016, May 2). *The other Islamic state: Al-Qaeda is still fighting for an emirate of its own*. Retrieved from PRI: http://www.pri.org/stories/2016-04-29/other-islamic-state-al-qaeda-still-fighting-emirate-its-ow

threat of punishment justified by their extreme and literal interpretation of religious texts and traditions.

In general, life under Jabhat Al-Nusra's rule is not necessarily more "preferred" than life under ISIL or under a dictatorship, but it is an interesting juxtaposition and one that must be made when analyzing these groups. In the spectrum of autocratic rule in the region, Al-Nusra's activities may be currently lies somewhere in the middle but most certainly not considered "liberal." While Al-Nusra's Al-Qaeda roots are undeniable, their repeated assurances to Syrians and the world at large that they are not Al-Qaeda and ISIL and therefore not targeting the West frames their behaviors and approach in a different light. Make no mistake, this Al-Nusra is a highly organized and well-armed and supplied militant organization whose roots and tactics stem from their Al-Qaeda past, but their ability to market themselves as "different" may very well benefit their operations in the long run in Syria, which is something that the West and other parties must take into consideration.

Chapter 5: International Responses

While most of the world media attention has been focused primarily on ISIL's activities over the past few years, Jabhat Al-Nusra continues to expand its territory and influence within Syria, and the group presents a very peculiar problem for the international community. The very complex relationship between the U.S. and Russia has played itself out once more in this conflict, with the U.S. and Russia hesitantly making moves in Syria without an actual all-out assault against the rebel groups, even as it seems increasingly necessary in the long run for the U.S. and Russia to cooperate in their battles against Al-Nusra and ISIL as these groups dig their heels in even further among the local populations in which they operate.

The Syrian government views Al-Nusra, in many ways, the same way it views other rebel forces within the country. For Assad, Al-Nusra is an excuse to use toward the international community to exercise more extreme violence against the population wherever his government feels resistance. This plays very well into Al-Nusra's favor, since their entire premise for existing frames them as "protectors" of the country against Assad's Alawi Shi'a regime. At Syria's request, the Russian military has become increasing involved in the Syrian Civil War as well, launching air campaigns against Jabhat Al-Nusra, ISIL, and other rebel groups. One of their goals is to separate Al-Nusra from the other militant groups in the area that it is attempting to build an alliance with, such as Ahrar Al-Sham.[37] Separating Al-Nusra delays their desired collaboration with other groups, ultimately weakening their efforts in the long run. Russia, however, is very careful in its interactions in Syria, as much as it is carrying out Assad's policies in the country.

Iran's place in the Syrian conflict has ironically been one of Russian and Syrian validation,

---

[37] Al Monitor. (2016, June 5). *Is Russia readying for the kill in Syria?* Retrieved from Al-Monitor: http://www.al-monitor.com/pulse/originals/2016/06/russia-syria-nusra-aleppo-qaeda-ypg-us-jihadi.htm

reiterating to the world that Al-Nusra, ISIL, and all of the resistance groups in the conflict are violent and bent on spreading an extremist ideology. Iran has worked with the Syrian government to provide military and intelligence support in the field alongside the Lebanese Shi'a militant group Hezbollah and Iraqi Shi'a militias.[38] Since ISIL began its trek through Syria and Iraq, it has called for an increase in lone wolf attacks around the world. The United States, Canada, and many European and Asian countries have now found themselves in a very similar situation to that of the Middle East and Africa, essentially hubs of Salafi extremist activities in the world. Iran's Revolutionary Guard Corps and Hezbollah have worked very closely with the Syrian forces on the ground in their fight against Al-Nusra and the other militant groups. Quoting an Iranian military official, *Al Monitor* notes, "In fact, the real danger for the US, and the West in general, isn't Daesh but [Jabhat al-] Nusra…It's really strange how history repeats itself." [39]

For the United States, Al-Nusra has become another nuisance to deal with in the region. The U.S. and Russian approaches to terrorism in Syria and Iraq has been likened to a game of whack-a-mole, shifting focuses between ISIL and other terrorist groups around the area. As ISIL's support and hold over their territory in Iraq and Syria has decreased, Al-Nusra's has arisen in Idlib and Aleppo. When Assad crossed the U.S. designated red-line by using chemical weapons against civilians in the summer of 2013, the U.S. put itself in a precarious position. During the beginning of the Arab Spring, the Obama Administration had tried to position itself as a supporter of protesters and rebel movements against the dictatorships around the region. However, when they failed to act in Syria after the extreme force of the Assad regime, the militias in the country took note, particularly Jabhat Al-Nusra. This collective international inaction was essentially the fuel Al-Nusra needed to build legitimacy with its base of supporters. They could now convincingly persuade the people that nobody else would come to their rescue. Al-Nusra aksi offered itself as an alternative to the international tension between the U.S. and Russia which held up immediate efforts to stop the violence.

During the build-up of ISIL-controlled territory in Iraq and Syria, the U.S. maintained efforts to destroy the group. There was even discussion among top leaders in the government to consider arming other groups—including Jabhat Al-Nusra—to fight against ISIL.[40] It was suggested and floated throughout the media that former CIA Director David Petraeus suggested supporting Al-Nusra against efforts ISIL because of his own experience funding militias in Iraq in 2007 when he was commander of the U.S. forces. Dealing with Al-Nusra, ISIL and other militant groups in the Syrian conflict has put the U.S. in a very difficult situation and one that also mirrors past behavior, particularly when it comes to funding militant groups.

---

[38] Fulton, W. J. (2013, May). *Iranian Strategy in Syria*. Retrieved from Institute for the Study of War: http://www.understandingwar.org/report/iranian-strategy-syria

[39] Hashem, A. (2016, April 15). *Iranian official says Nusra, not IS, main threat to West*. Retrieved from Al-Monitor: http://www.al-monitor.com/pulse/originals/2016/04/iran-syria-palmyra-nusrah-islamic-state.htm

[40] Harris, S. a. (2015, August 31). *Petraeus: Use Al Qaeda Fighters to Beat ISIS*. Retrieved from The Daily Beast: http://www.thedailybeast.com/articles/2015/08/31/petraeus-use-al-qaeda-fighters-to-beat-isis.htm

Petraeus

The Cold War-like approach of the U.S. and Russia has left analysts and policymakers befuddled. Analysts note that following the end of the Cold War in the late 1980s, there has been an overall decrease in international conflicts and global conflicts but a rise in civil wars around the world, as various religious, ethnic, and nationalist groups attempt to throw off the yoke of the residual effects of colonialism. In Syria, much like in other countries around the developing world, there is a long-term secular military dictator who has shown preference to some groups (Shi'a, Christians) over others (Sunnis), thus causing an upset in the balance in the region. Many analysts believe that the protests and upheaval like the Middle East experience during the Arab Spring was a long-time coming, but it was difficult to really anticipate the full extent of the chaos that ensued. The moment seemed ripe in international relations: a deadly mix of rising tension among the world's superpowers (United States, Russia), global economic problems, a steadily rising youth population, and an increase in non-state actor violent movements around the world. The Cold War may be over, but the world is still very much in the throes of a distinct phase in a new world defined asymmetric warfare between national militaries and small militant groups.

Chapter 6: Financing and Supporting the Jihad

Militant groups cannot survive without sources of funding. Throughout Jabhat Al-Nusra's existence, Al-Qaeda has been fairly explicit in its support for the operations in Syria. Osama Bin Laden, himself a Saudi, made several connections during his time and through his own recruitment efforts. "The main group of donors is based in the Gulf area, principally Saudi Arabia, but donors also exist in other parts of the world. Some of these donors have been fully aware of the final destination of their money; others were not."[41]

An American leaflet showing Bin Laden and Zawahiri

Since the wars of colonial revolution of the 1940s and onwards in the Middle East and others parts of the Muslim world, the countries of the Arabian Gulf—Saudi Arabia, Qatar, Kuwait, and the United Arab Emirates—emerged as potential sources of funding for terrorist groups in the region. This information is not new and definitely not surprising to anyone who paid close attention to the region for some time. The leaders of the Gulf countries essentially came to power due to their ability to mix Wahabbi Islam with modern autocracy. What has emerged are several kingdoms (or "emirates") controlled by ruling families which are very much influenced by conservative Islam whose rules are mandated and enforced throughout their countries. There have been numerous reports over the years of these countries actively funding and supporting terrorist groups around the world.

For Jabhat Al-Nusra, resources in many cases have taken the form of previously used weapons

---

[41] del Cid Gómez, J. M. (2010). *A Financial Profile of the Terrorism of Al-Qaeda and its Affiliates.* Retrieved from Perspective on Terrorism: http://www.terrorismanalysts.com/pt/index.php/pot/article/view/113/htm

[42] Karouny, M: (2015, March 4). *Insight - Syria's Nusra Front may leave Qaeda to form new entity.* Retrieved from Reuters: http://uk.reuters.com/article/uk-mideast-crisis-nusra-insight-idUKKBN0M00G620150304

that were already purchased by Al-Qaeda or those that they have taken during their battles within Syria. In 2015, some sources reported that Qatar was encouraging Al-Nusra to break away from Al-Qaeda and operate independently.[42] These sources report discussions between Abu Muhammad Al-Julani and officials from Qatar and other Gulf states. These reports are ironic, given the fact that Qatar, Saudi Arabia, Bahrain and the U.A.E. are part of the coalition to defeat ISIL, though they actually only operate exclusively inside of Syria.

A Sunni-backed opposition to Bashar Assad would be ideal for the Gulf; political scientists view the entire region as a balancing act, each side teetering toward Shi'ism or Sunnism. Assad's strongest backer is Iran, a Shi'a majority country that has no qualms about stating its opinion on the treatment of Shi'ites and Sunnis in the Gulf and around the world. The Obama Administration has tried over the last few years to ease tensions with Iran through a few highly publicized meetings and the negotiations over Iran's nuclear program, but while relations between the two countries have not changed much, the reaction from the Gulf countries has not been positive. These countries may feel that an easing in tension between the U.S. and Iran may have real impact on the region, eventually tipping the balance once again in Iran's favor. With this in mind, the Middle East's richest leaders would certainly be concerned about their part in preventing a Shi'a takeover. These very same fears are the same reason Qatar, Kuwait, Saudi Arabia and others have supported various militant groups over time in the region. When the Syrian Civil War began, the Gulf took notice and was perhaps even more interested in the eventual outcome of the conflict than perhaps even the U.S. and Russia.

The leaders of Turkey have also made statements nearly indicating support of Al-Nusra's efforts. Since the outset of the war, Turkey has had a vested interest in the fate of its neighbor to the south. During the early days of the conflict when analysts and politicians believed it would end just as quickly as the rebellions around the region, Turkey had supported the Muslim Brotherhood in Syria in hopes that they would take control in a post-Assad country. When that did not work out, there were reports that Turkey—like Qatar—reached out to Al-Nusra about a partnership. Ideally, this partnership would be a good balance to the Kurds in Syria that are allied with the Kurdish Workers Party (PKK), Turkey's long-time domestic militant group.[43] While Turkey has not admitted to giving financial support to Al-Nusra, there are reports that they permit safe passage of supplies to Al-Nusra through its borders from the Gulf.[44] The group appears to be one of convenience for Turkey.

As Dr. David Roberts put it in a BBC article on the matter, "Qatar has surmised, it seems, that supporting or transforming the Nusra Front, is one of the 'least worst' options."[45] As mentioned above, the U.S. even thought that way at one point as well. Supporting Al-Nusra is certainly not

[43] Stein, A. (2015, February 9). *Turkey's Evolving Syria Strategy*. Retrieved from Foreign Affairs:
    https://www.foreignaffairs.com/articles/turkey/2015-02-09/turkeys-evolving-syria-strategy
[44] Ibid
[45] Roberts, D. D. (2015, March 6). *Is Qatar bringing the Nusra Front in from the cold?* Retrieved from BBC News:
    http://www.bbc.com/news/world-middle-east-31764114

a perfect option by any means, but since they have already begun to build strong supporting among the population and have been relatively well-resourced, Qatar, Turkey, and other would-be supporters assume that Al-Nusra will be the only organized Sunni group still standing when the dust settles after the war. At this stage, there is no way of knowing if that will be the case, especially with the United States and Russia considering changing their approach to the civil war overall. What does appear to remain true is that Jabhat Al-Nusra has positioned itself as very much "the lesser of two evils" in juxtaposition to ISIL. The leaders of the Sunni countries in the region are looking for a champion to keep their own interests afloat during the chaos, but it is uncertain whether or not Al-Nusra is a group to be tamed or one to be supported from afar, much like Hezbollah's relationship with Iran.

Chapter 7: Rebranding Jabhat Al-Nusra

In July 2016, Abu Muhammad Al-Julani announced that Jabhat Al-Nusra would formally split from Al-Qaeda and change its name to Jabhat Fatah Al-Sham, or "The Front for the Conquest of the Levant."[46] Al-Julani indicated that the name change was meant to further encourage unification of Syrian militant and revolutionary groups under one umbrella. By focusing on collaboration among Syrian fighters, Al-Nusra aims to position itself once again as a group whose sole focus is to protect the Syrian Sunni population and topple Bashar Assad's regime.

It's apparent that by continuing to be connected to Al-Qaeda--and ISIL often referenced to in its past--Al-Nusra believed its ability to appeal more broadly to Syrians was limited. A few days prior to this statement, Al-Qaeda confirmed that the group split officially.[47] In the days following Al-Julani's announcements, various Al-Qaeda affiliated groups and leaders lauded the split from Al-Qaeda, which begs the question of why the split would be a good thing for Al-Qaeda in the first place.

U.S. officials and some experts believe that this name change and rebranding is an effort to avoid affiliation with other Western-country designated terrorist groups in hopes that they might receive support from the U.S. and others in their efforts against the Syrian regime.[48] After all, for all intents and purposes, there is no reason to believe that their tactics and approach to the civil war will be any different. Al-Nusra apparently views its current situation as a prime opportunity to consolidate power in the areas that it controls. The reaction from other militant groups in Syria seems generally positive to the break with Al-Qaeda, though there has been little indication that a larger merger of any kind is currently taking place.[49] There is likely some misapprehension because the split can be viewed with skepticism among would-be allies and long-time enemies,

[46] Al Jazeera. (2016, July 29). *Al-Nusra leader Jolanie announces split from Al-Qaeda*. Retrieved from Al Jazeera: http://www.aljazeera.com/news/2016/07/al-nusra-leader-jolani-announces-split-al-qaeda-160728163725624.htm
[47] Ibid
[48] Sanchez, R. a. (2016, August 1). *Syria's al-Nusra rebrands and cuts ties with al Qaeda*. Retrieved from CNN: http://www.cnn.com/2016/07/28/middleeast/al-nusra-al-qaeda-split
[49] *Opinions Divided on Nusra's Split from Al-Qaeda*. Retrieved from News Deeply: https://www.newsdeeply.com/syria/articles/2016/08/09/opinions-divided-on-nusras-split-from-al-qaida

particularly since Al-Qaeda has financially and logistically supported Al-Nusra from its inception.

As experts look at the various reactions to the split in the days following the announcements, it is not hard to understand why most do not believe the Al-Qaeda split is anything more than a publicity stunt. Many of the leading Syrian militant groups have stated their hesitation to merge with Al-Nusra due to their affiliation with Al-Qaeda. The fear was that this would lead to justification among Russian and U.S. airstrikes.[50] By publicly separating from Al-Qaeda, Al-Nusra is hoping to finally realize its ultimate goal of uniting factions under its control and eventually leading to a larger, more concerted effort to finally bring down Bashar Assad's regime. The merging of terrorist groups has definitely happened before, but inevitably the issue of leadership comes to the forefront as varying personalities begin vying for control. Abu Muhammad Al-Julani and his leadership team are no doubt considering this future issue for whenever groups merge into their own. It will either be a fruitful exercise in power sharing among the jihadists or will turn out much like Al-Nusra's own origins, when ISIL split from Al-Qaeda due to a personality and ideology clash between Abu Bakr Al-Baghdadi and Al-Qaeda leadership.

Through it all, Jabhat Al-Nusra's rise to control in Syria has been a peculiar mix of learning from Al-Qaeda's past mistakes and innovative approaches to recruitment reflecting the shift of jihadist organizations to using social media tools. While it started out as a cell of Al-Qaeda in Iraq (AQI) sent by Abu Bakr Al-Baghdadi to Syria to carry out operations in the early days of the Syrian Civil War, it has since grown into a respected, well-established and well-resourced jihadist movement on the battleground, both offline and online. Al-Nusra's makeup of predominantly Syrian fighters led by more seasoned jihadists from former Al-Qaeda operations in central Asia and around the Middle East has helped it to establish its firm and credible hold in some key locations around Syria, such as Idlib and Deir Al-Zour. Having a majority of the fighters as native Syrians has helped to assuage the fears of locals that the force is actually foreign with an agenda unconcerned with Syrian long-term stability. Al-Nusra's formal breakaway from ISIL in 2013 and from Al-Qaeda and 2016 is part of a larger attempt to slowly but surely move toward positioning itself as an entirely native operation.

Life under Al-Nusra's control is not entirely similar to that of ISIL in Iraq, as their tactics remain seemingly less harsh in comparison. In most cases, Al-Nusra works with the community leadership in the areas that it controls and implements various services, such as food delivery, medical care, and education all the while providing "protection" against the Syrian government's army. As part of their vision of protection against the Assad regime, they have instituted religious academies for recruiting and training young children to develop into jihadist fighters. They have also begun to increase the presence of religious police throughout their territory to

[50] Zimmerman, K. a. (2016, July 28). *Avoiding al Qaeda's Syria trap: Jabhat al Nusra's rebranding.* Retrieved from AEI: https://www.aei.org/publication/avoiding-al-qaedas-syria-trap-jabhat-al-nusras-rebranding

command adherence to their interpretation of strict Sunni religious law. All of these behaviors are similar in practice to Sunni jihadi movements around the world, especially since their ultimate aim is to establish an Islamic caliphate that controls every movement and practice of the population. The name change and recent dissociation from Al-Qaeda appear to indicate a shift in tactics. Al-Nusra leaders seem to believe that they are moving toward a ripe moment in which merging with other militant groups will bring the group to the next level of legitimacy and support among their Sunni base, even if the other militant groups remain hesitant as they have no real proof or reason to believe that Al-Nusra is not still backed by Al-Qaeda.

Meanwhile, the international community's response to the Syrian Civil War has definitely left much to be desired. The United States and Russia have once again found themselves embroiled in another conflict through proxies on the battlefield. They are each being forced to confront each other on a foreign battlefield and deal with the global backlash at home and abroad for their actions. Moreover, since the Arab Spring and rise of ISIL, there has been an increase in lone wolf attacks around the world. These attacks cause distraction in the media and among Western populations who feel even less inclined to engage with the Muslim world and welcome the ensuing waves of refugees fleeing the conflict for Europe and North America. With these complexities comes a very difficult situation for the United States. As much as it wants to get involved in the Syrian conflict and put its policy stances into action and even ponder backing Al-Nusra in efforts against ISIL and the Syrian government, Russian support for the Assad regime and Iranian and Hezbollah involvement have created a stalemate. When President Obama gave his famous "red line" speech in the summer of 2013 regarding Assad's use of chemical weapons against Syria and then failed to act when the attacks actually took place, Jabhat Al-Nusra capitalized on the situation. Repeated inaction and seemingly aimless foreign policy stances on the Syrian Civil War have played in to Al-Nusra's favor.

As much as Al-Nusra may try to show the world it is different from its rivals (particularly ISIL and now Al-Qaeda) in the region, their ideology and goals suggest otherwise. Regardless, Jabhat Al-Nusra is definitely a serious force to be reckoned with and one that the world should pay more attention to, especially as ISIL continues to be put on the defensive in Syria and Iraq. Al-Nusra is very much like Hezbollah, Hamas, and the Muslim Brotherhood in the sense that their ability to entrench themselves locally will likely assist them in the long-run. With this in mind, they may be able to turn themselves into a Muslim Brotherhood-like political, albeit armed, Islamist force in the eventual negotiations that will take place in Syria. Al-Nusra may then be able to gather supporters under its banner in the new Syrian society. Thus, if and when a post-Bashar Assad Syria finally comes to pass, Al-Nusra will definitely be a concern for the world during reconstruction efforts in the region.

Online Resources

Other books about Middle Eastern history by Charles River Editors

Other books about the Nusra Front on Amazon

Bibliography

Abbas, Y. (2016, May 10). How Al-Qaeda is Winning in Syria. Retrieved from War on the Rocks: http://warontherocks.com/2016/05/how-al-qaeda-is-winning-in-syria/

Al Jazeera. (2016, July 29). Al-Nusra leader Jolanie announces split from Al-Qaeda. Retrieved from Al Jazeera: http://www.aljazeera.com/news/2016/07/al-nusra-leader-jolani-announces-split-al-qaeda-160728163725624.html

A-Monitor. (2016, June 5). Is Russia readying for the kill in Syria? Retrieved from Al-Monitor: http://www.al-monitor.com/pulse/originals/2016/06/russia-syria-nusra-aleppo-qaeda-ypg-us-jihadi.html

Barna, C. (2014). The Road to Jihad in Syria: Using SOCMINT to Counter the Radicalization of Muslim Youth in Romania. In M. Lombardi, E. Ragab, V. Chin, Y. Dandurand, V. de Divitiis, & A. Burato, Countering Radicalisation and Youth Extremism Among Youth to Prevent Terrorism. Milan: IOS Press.

BBC News. (2014, September 24). What is the Khorasan Group? Retrieved from BBC New: http://www.bbc.com/news/world-middle-east-29350271

BBC News. (2015, May 28). Al-Qaeda 'orders Syria's Al-Nusra Front not to attack West'. Retrieved from BBC News: http://www.bbc.com/news/world-middle-east-32913509

Benotman, N. a. (n.d.). Jabhat Al-Nusra: A Strategic Briefing. Retrieved from Quilliam Foundation: https://web.archive.org/web/20150328080133/http://www.quilliamfoundation.org/wp/wp-content/uploads/publications/free/jabhat-al-nusra-a-strategic-briefing.pdf

Byman, D. L. (2015, February 24). ISIS vs. Al Qaeda: Jihadism's global civil war. Retrieved from Brookings Institution: https://www.brookings.edu/articles/isis-vs-al-qaeda-jihadisms-global-civil-war/

Daireh, M. (2015, November 11). Inside the Battle: Al Nusra-Al Qaeda in Syria. Retrieved from VICE News: https://news.vice.com/video/inside-the-battle-al-nusra-al-qaeda-in-syria

del Cid Gómez, J. M. (2010). A Financial Profile of the Terrorism of Al-Qaeda and its Affiliates. Retrieved from Perspective on Terrorism: http://www.terrorismanalysts.com/pt/index.php/pot/article/view/113/html

Fanack - Chronicle. (2015, July 1). Jabhat Al-Nusra Tries to Look Like a Moderate Terrorist Group. Retrieved from Fanack - Chronicle of the Middle East & North Africa:

https://chronicle.fanack.com/specials/extremism/jabhat-al-nusra-tries-to-look-a-moderate-terrorist-group/

Farag, N. (2014). Between Piety and Politics: Social Services and the Muslim Brotherhood. Retrieved from Frontline - PBS: http://www.pbs.org/wgbh/pages/frontline/revolution-in-cairo/inside-muslim-brotherhood/piety-and-politics.html

Fulton, W. J. (2013, May). Iranian Strategy in Syria. Retrieved from Institute for the Study of War: http://www.understandingwar.org/report/iranian-strategy-syria

Gartenstein-Ross, D. a. (2013, August 22). How Syria's Jihadists Win Friends and Influence People. Retrieved from The Atlantic: http://www.theatlantic.com/international/archive/2013/08/how-syrias-jihadists-win-friends-and-influence-people/278942/

Habeck, M. (2014, June 27). Assessing the ISIS - Al-Qaeda Split: The Origins of the Dispute. Retrieved from Insite Blog on Terrorism & Extremism: http://news.siteintelgroup.com/blog/index.php/categories/jihad/entry/193-assessing-the-isis-al-qaeda-split-the-origins-of-the-dispute-1

Haid, H. (2016, August 9). Opinions Divided on Nusra's Split from Al-Qaeda. Retrieved from News Deeply: https://www.newsdeeply.com/syria/articles/2016/08/09/opinions-divided-on-nusras-split-from-al-qaida

Hall, R. a. (2016, May 2). The other Islamic state: Al-Qaeda is still fighting for an emirate of its own. Retrieved from PRI: http://www.pri.org/stories/2016-04-29/other-islamic-state-al-qaeda-still-fighting-emirate-its-own

Harris, S. a. (2015, August 31). Petraeus: Use Al Qaeda Fighters to Beat ISIS. Retrieved from The Daily Beast: http://www.thedailybeast.com/articles/2015/08/31/petraeus-use-al-qaeda-fighters-to-beat-isis.html

Hashem, A. (2016, April 15). Iranian official says Nusra, not IS, main threat to West. Retrieved from Al-Monitor: http://www.al-monitor.com/pulse/originals/2016/04/iran-syria-palmyra-nusrah-islamic-state.html

How Jabhat Al Nusra Uses Twitter to Spread Propaganda. (2016, May 4). Retrieved from VOX Pol: http://www.voxpol.eu/how-jabhat-al-nusra-uses-twitter-to-spread-propaganda/

Internet World Stats. (2015, November). Internet Usage in the Middle East. Retrieved from Internet World Stats: http://www.Internetworldstats.com/stats5.htm

Karouny, M. (2015, March 4). Insight - Syria's Nusra Front may leave Qaeda to form new entity. Retrieved from Reuters: http://uk.reuters.com/article/uk-mideast-crisis-nusra-insight-idUKKBN0M00G620150304

Montgomery, K. (2015, April 13). Jabhat Al Nusra: A Game Change in Syria. Retrieved from World Policy Blog: http://www.worldpolicy.org/blog/2015/04/13/jabhat-al-nusra-game-changer-syri

Prucha, N. a. (2013, June 25). Tweeting for the Caliphate: Twitter as the New Frontier for Jihadist Propaganda. Retrieved from Combating Terrorist Center at West Point: https://www.ctc.usma.edu/posts/tweeting-for-the-caliphate-twitter-as-the-new-frontier-for-jihadist-propaganda

Roberts, D. D. (2015, March 6). Is Qatar bringing the Nusra Front in from the cold? Retrieved from BBC News: http://www.bbc.com/news/world-middle-east-31764114

Roggio, B. (2006, October 16). The Rump Islamic Emirate of Iraq. Retrieved from The Long War Journal: http://www.longwarjournal.org/archives/2006/10/the_rump_islamic_emi.php#

Sanchez, R. a. (2016, August 1). Syria's al-Nusra rebrands and cuts ties with al Qaeda. Retrieved from CNN: http://www.cnn.com/2016/07/28/middleeast/al-nusra-al-qaeda-split/

Schatz, B. (2016, August 5). Meet the Terrorist Group Playing the Long Game in Syria. Retrieved from MotherJones: http://www.motherjones.com/politics/2016/08/syria-al-qaeda-nusra-battle-aleppo

Stein, A. (2015, February 9). Turkey's Evolving Syria Strategy. Retrieved from Foreign Affairs: https://www.foreignaffairs.com/articles/turkey/2015-02-09/turkeys-evolving-syria-strategy

yalibnan. (2015, March 19). Al Qaeda forces Druze of Idlib Syria to destory their shrines and convert. Retrieved from YaLibnan: http://yalibnan.com/2015/03/19/al-qaeda-forces-druze-of-idlib-syria-to-destroy-their-shrines-and-convert/

Zimmerman, K. a. (2016, July 28). Avoiding al Qaeda's Syria trap: Jabhat al Nusra's rebranding. Retrieved from AEI: https://www.aei.org/publication/avoiding-al-qaedas-syria-trap-jabhat-al-nusras-rebranding/

Free Books by Charles River Editors

We have brand new titles available for free most days of the week. To see which of our titles are currently free, click on this link.

Discounted Books by Charles River Editors

We have titles at a discount price of just 99 cents everyday. To see which of our titles are currently 99 cents, click on this link.

18585053R00027

Printed in Poland
by Amazon Fulfillment
Poland Sp. z o.o., Wrocław